Condition of vegetation communities in Delaware Water Gap National Recreation Area:

Eastern Rivers and Mountains Network summary report 2007–2009

Natural Resource Data Series NPS/ERMN/NRDS—2010/037

Stephanie J. Perles, Kristina K. Callahan, and Matthew R. Marshall

National Park Service
Northeast Region
Eastern Rivers and Mountains Network
Forest Resources Building
University Park, Pennsylvania 16802

March 2010

U.S. Department of the Interior
National Park Service
Natural Resource Program Center
Fort Collins, Colorado

The National Park Service, Natural Resource Program Center publishes a range of reports that address natural resource topics of interest and applicability to a broad audience in the National Park Service and others in natural resource management, including scientists, conservation and environmental constituencies, and the public.

The Natural Resource Data Series is intended for timely release of basic data sets and data summaries. Care has been taken to assure accuracy of raw data values, but a thorough analysis and interpretation of the data has not been completed. Consequently, the initial analyses of data in this report are provisional and subject to change.

All manuscripts in the series receive the appropriate level of peer review to ensure that the information is scientifically credible, technically accurate, appropriately written for the intended audience, and designed and published in a professional manner. Data in this report were collected and analyzed using methods based on established, peer-reviewed protocols and were analyzed and interpreted within the guidelines of the protocols.

Views, statements, findings, conclusions, recommendations, and data in this report are those of the author(s) and do not necessarily reflect views and policies of the National Park Service, U.S. Department of the Interior. Mention of trade names or commercial products does not constitute endorsement or recommendation for use by the National Park Service.

This report is available from the Eastern Rivers and Mountains Network website (http://science.nature.nps.gov/im/units/ERMN) and the Natural Resource Publications Management website (http://www.nature.nps.gov/publications/NRPM).

Please cite this publication as:

Perles, S. J., K. K. Callahan, and M. R. Marshall. 2010. Condition of vegetation communities in Delaware Water Gap National Recreation Area: Eastern Rivers and Mountains Network summary report 2007–2009. Natural Resource Data Series NPS/ERMN/NRDS—2010/037. National Park Service, Fort Collins, Colorado.

NPS 620/101469, March 2010

Contents

Figures

Tables

Executive Summary

Beginning in 2007, the Eastern Rivers and Mountains Network (ERMN) of the National Park Service (NPS) began monitoring vegetation communities and soil in eight of its nine parks. The objective of this monitoring program is to provide information on the condition of the parks' vegetation and soil and how this condition is changing through time. Thus far, 77 permanent long-term monitoring plots have been established in Delaware Water Gap National Recreation Area (DEWA). Within the permanent plots, data are collected on forest stand structure; tree health, growth, and mortality; tree regeneration; coarse woody debris; shrubs; groundstory diversity; invasive species; and soil. The last panel of plots will be established in 2010, and in 2011 the first panel of plots will be revisited, providing data on how the vegetation is changing through time.

This report summarizes vegetation monitoring data collected between 2007 and 2009 in DEWA and presents the condition of the park's vegetation based on those data. These data provide a snap-shot of the status of the vegetation communities and are compared to expected ranges of variability for eastern forests. The results reported here provide highlights of the available data, but additional measures are being investigated and may be reported in the future.

Vegetation condition highlights within DEWA include:

- Forest stands within the park are predominantly young or middle-aged.

- In the park's dry forest types, the trees that are regenerating (trees of the future) are not the same species as are present in the canopy (present trees). Despite the dominance of oaks in the canopy, oaks are underrepresented in the sapling layer, which is dominated by white pine, red maple, and black birch. Oaks also make up a disproportionately smaller percentage of the seedling layer, which is predominantly maples, shadbush, and black birch. If this trend continues, the park's dry forests will contain fewer oaks and more red maple, white pine, and black birch in the future.

- Between 22–65% of the forested plots currently contain insufficient tree regeneration to replace the forest canopy, depending on the intensity of deer browse pressure.

- Jack-in-the-pulpit and Canada mayflower are the most abundant species that are being monitored as indicators of deer browse pressure. Changes in the number of plants, their height, and their reproductive status are being monitored and will be reported in the future.

- Three common forest pests documented in the plots are gypsy moth, hemlock woolly adelgid, and elongate hemlock scale. Gypsy moth abundance peaked in 2008, with 88% of forested plots containing gypsy moths or their caterpillars that year.

- Snag (standing dead trees) densities and the volume of coarse woody debris (fallen logs) are typical of values found in other second-growth forests in the eastern United States. Snags and coarse woody debris provide important habitat for wildlife.

- The most common and abundant shrubs in moist habitats in the park are exotic invasive species, including multiflora rose, Japanese barberry, honeysuckles, and autumn olive. In dry habitats, native ericaceous shrubs such as blueberries, huckleberries, Mountain laurel, and scrub oak are the most common species.

- In the groundstory of dry habitats, native species contribute the vast majority of the species richness and cover. In moist habitats, native species account for about two-thirds of the species richness and cover, while nonnative species account for the remaining one-third of richness and cover.

- Only 39% of the plots are free of invasive plant species, while 43% of the plots contain three or more invasive plant species.

- Six early detections of two new exotic invasive species were documented by the vegetation monitoring field crews between 2008 and 2009. The locations of the new exotic invasive species were reported to park natural resource managers and at least one of these populations was eradicated. Based on these observations, viburnum leaf beetle is wide-spread in the Flat Brook valley and has already caused significant dieback in the native viburnum shrubs there. Narrowleaf bittercress has been found in several places along the floodplain of the Delaware River and will likely be a significant invader in these moist habitats in the next few years.

In general, forests in DEWA are typical of other second-growth forests in the Appalachian Mountains; however, results from the monitoring data underscore two important points for park managers:

1) **Invasive exotic plant species are a pervasive and spreading threat to the park's vegetation communities**. This finding underscores the vital importance of the many ongoing projects in DEWA directed by park managers, external researchers, and the Exotic Pest Management Teams that are addressing invasive exotic plants. When possible, additional resources should be strategically allocated to managing invasive exotic species by:
   a) managing invasive exotic plants in sensitive, rare habitats.
   b) detecting and eliminating (when possible) new populations of invasive exotic species novel to the park (implementation of the Early Detection and Rapid Response protocol).
   c) working with partners to acquire and release approved biological controls for invasive exotic species that are widespread and abundant in the park.

2) **The factors contributing to poor tree regeneration, particularly of oaks, need to be investigated further in order to evaluate potential management actions**. This regeneration failure could be attributed to one or more of the following factors: dense shade from canopy or subcanopy trees; competition from shrubs, ferns, or grasses; altered disturbance regimes, including fire suppression, browse pressure from white-tailed deer, and/or soil infertility. As more data on both vegetation and soil are collected from the monitoring plots we will investigate correlations between these factors discussed and tree regeneration in DEWA. We hope to be able to provide guidance on potential management actions pertaining to forest regeneration.

Introduction

In 2007, the Eastern Rivers and Mountains Network (ERMN) of the National Park Service (NPS) began monitoring vegetation communities and soil in eight of its nine parks. This monitoring effort is a component of the ERMN Vital Signs monitoring program (Marshall and Piekielek 2007) as part of the nationwide NPS Inventory and Monitoring Program (Fancy et al. 2009).

Long-term monitoring of vegetation and soils was identified among the highest priority vital signs during the ERMN prioritization process (Marshall and Piekielek 2007). The vital sign process highlighted the importance of plant species diversity and functional plant communities as natural resources critical to the parks. These vegetation communities also serve as an integrated measure of terrestrial ecosystem health by expressing information about climate, soils, and disturbance. Furthermore, vegetation serves as a base for other trophic components such as wildlife.

The ERMN Vegetation and Soil Monitoring Program provides information regarding the condition of the park's vegetation and soil and how this condition is changing through time. Data generated by this program contribute to the monitoring of several of the network's vital signs, including: Forest, Woodland, Shrubland, and Riparian Plant Communities; Status and Trends of Invasive/Exotic Plants, Animals, and Diseases; Early Detection of Invasive/Exotic Plants, Animals, and Diseases; and Soil Function and Dynamics.

Numerous ecological and anthropogenic forces affect the park's vegetation. Ecological factors such as geology, soil nutrient availability, weather, and disturbance patterns directly influence the structure, composition, and dynamics of the vegetation. Some anthropogenic stressors are easily identified, such as visitor overuse or loss and fragmentation of habitat due to development inside and outside of the parks. Many changes in forest vegetation through time are often linked to several interacting ecological and anthropogenic factors. Exotic species, white-tailed deer (*Odocoileus virginianus*), atmospheric acid and nutrient deposition, climate change, altered disturbance regimes, and changes in land use are also important factors affecting the park's vegetation (Rentch 2006, Perles et al. 2009).

Depending on the successional stage, disturbance history, and site conditions, there are certain parameters within which a terrestrial vegetation ecosystem can be described as "healthy" (Tierney et al 2009). By measuring taxonomic, structural, and demographic features, an assessment can be made as to whether or not the ecosystem's parameters fall within expected or accepted norms and ranges of variability. These measures serve as indicators of ecological integrity that can be explicitly linked to park management.

This report is intended to provide preliminary results to natural resource managers at Delaware Water Gap National Recreation Area (DEWA) on the condition of the vegetation communities in the park, utilizing the first three years' of collected data. These data provide a snap-shot of the status of the vegetation communities and are compared to expected ranges of variability for eastern forests. In the future, when the monitoring plots have been revisited, data will be available on how the vegetation is changing through time and these results will also be presented.

Methods

Although a brief overview of the vegetation and soil monitoring methods is provided here, a detailed rationale of the sampling design and methods, in addition to Standard Operating Procedures, are provided in the Vegetation and Soil Monitoring Protocol (Perles et al. 2009). The protocol was based on the U.S. Forest Service (USFS) Forest Inventory and Analysis (FIA) program (USFS 2007) and the vegetation monitoring protocols of four other Inventory and Monitoring programs in the eastern United States (Sanders et al. 2006, Schmit et al. 2006, Tierney and Faber-Langendoen 2007, Comisky et al. 2009). Adopting widely used protocols facilitates comparisons of ERMN data with other NPS networks and regional data sets.

Site Selection

Vegetation and soil are monitored at permanent plots, since the use of permanent plots increases power to detect trends through time. For each park, a regular grid of potential plot locations was overlain on the park. Sampling locations were selected from the regular grid using a generalized random-tessellation stratified (GRTS) design (McDonald 2004, Stevens and Olsen 2004). The three main advantages to a GRTS design are: 1) the GRTS design is spatially balanced, wherein there is generally uniform dispersion of sampling sites over the area of interest; 2) the GRTS design allows for flexible sample size, such that sites can be added to or excluded from the sampling plan without compromising the integrity of the overall design; and 3) the GRTS method is a probabilistic sampling design, whereby sampling points are randomly chosen from among those in a systematic grid, eliminating site selection bias, and allowing inference to the entire sampling frame (Stevens and Olsen 2004).

Plots are sampled on a four-year panel design, in which one panel containing one-fourth of a park's total plots is sampled each year. On the fifth year, the first panel is re-sampled. Sampling began in DEWA in 2007. Over the past three summers, a total of 77 plots have been sampled; 26 plots in 2007, 26 plots in 2008, and 25 plots in 2009 (Figure 1). Sampling took place in June and the beginning of July each summer.

Field Methods

At each plot, the ERMN monitors a suite of vegetation and soil variables. The plot design includes several embedded sampling units (Figure 2). Tree, stand, and site measurements are collected within fixed-area, circular plots, 15 m in radius. Tree regeneration and shrub measurements are collected on four 2-m radius circular microplots embedded within each plot. Data on coarse woody debris are collected using line intersect sampling (Van Wagner 1964) along six 15-m transects. Data on understory plant composition and the diversity of understory species are monitored using twelve 1-m^2 quadrats set along the six transects. A photograph of the plot is taken from the plot's southern edge to document change in vegetation structure through time. Three soil samples are collected from sampling frames located adjacent to the plot's northern edge.

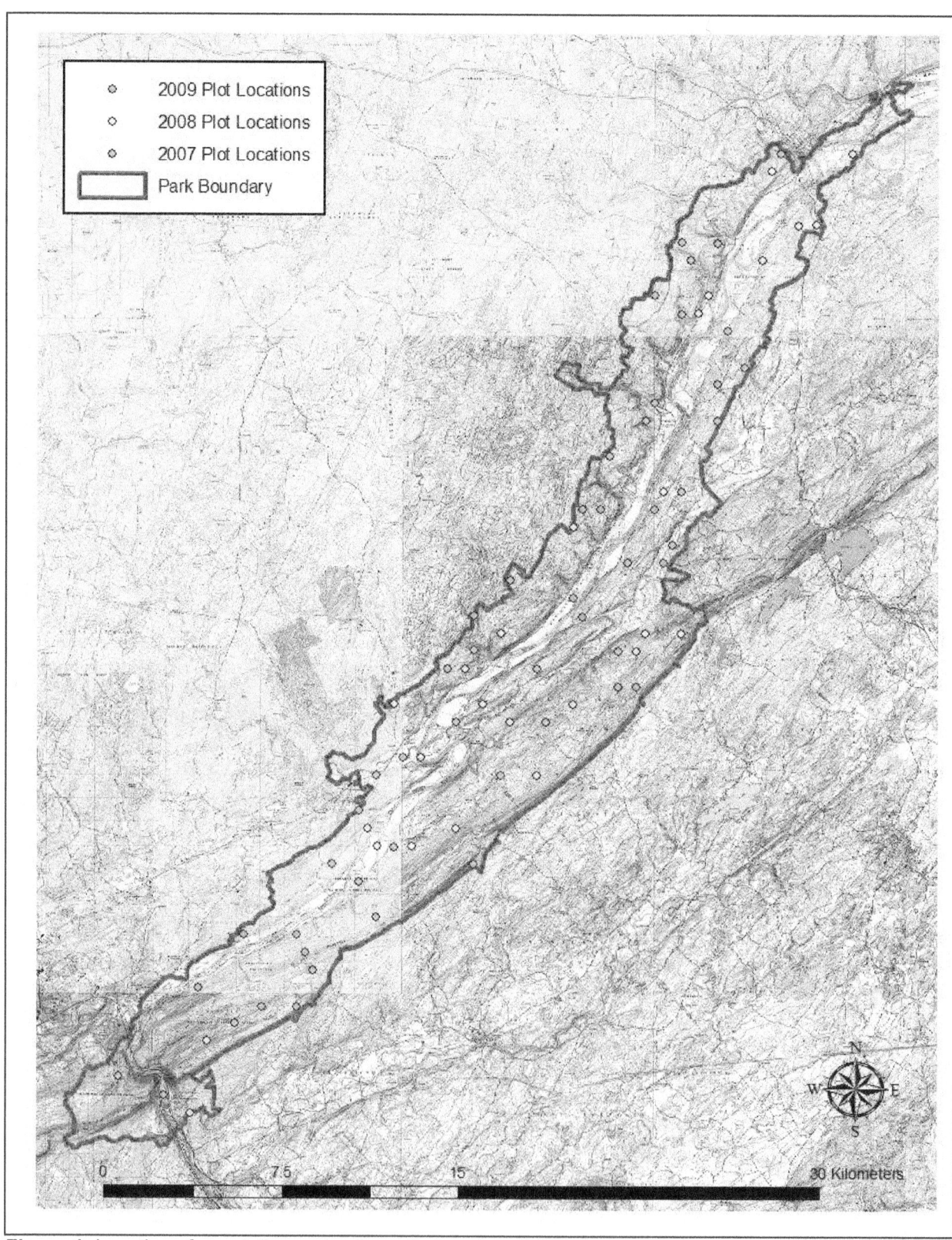

Figure 1. Location of vegetation and soil monitoring plots (2007–2009) in Delaware Water Gap National Recreation Area.

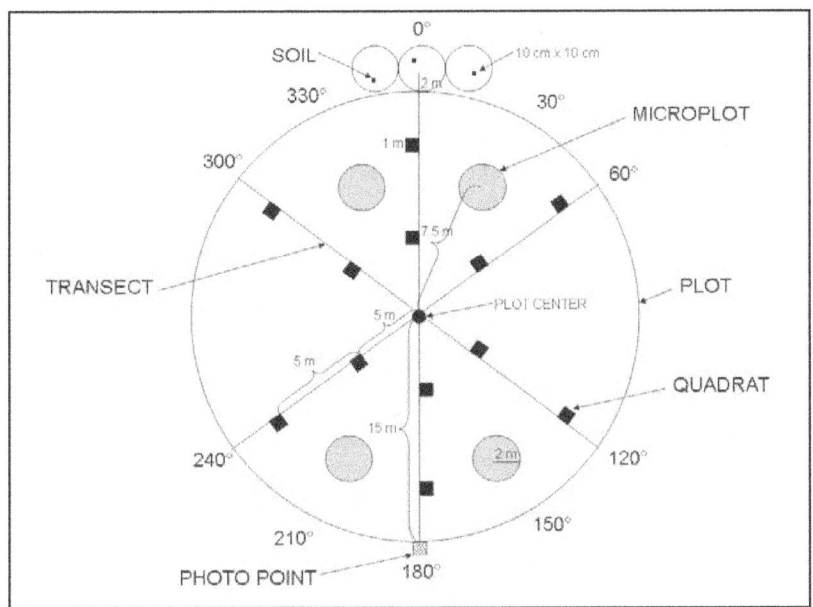

Figure 2. Plot design for Eastern Rivers and Mountains Network Vegetation Monitoring protocol. Tree, stand, and site measurements are collected within the plot. Tree regeneration and shrub measurements are collected in the microplots. Data on coarse woody debris are collected along the transects. Data on understory plant composition and the diversity of understory species are collected in the quadrats. A photograph of the plot is taken from the plot's southern edge. Three soil samples are collected from sampling frames located adjacent to the plot's northern edge.

Data Analysis

This report summarizes the vegetation monitoring data collected between 2007 and 2009 in DEWA and presents the condition of the park's vegetation based on those data. These data provide a snap-shot of the status of the vegetation communities and are compared to expected ranges of variability for eastern forests.

The results reported here are highlights of the available data, but additional measures are being investigated and may be reported in the future. Furthermore, as plots are revisited through time and additional data are collected, we will report how the conditions discussed below are changing through time.

Results

Stand Structure and Succession

The park's vegetation is primarily forest, though the forest stands vary greatly in age and land use history. A wide variety of non-forested vegetation types also exist in the park. Monitoring the successional stage of the vegetation plots provides a picture of the shifting mosaic of stand structures within the park. Based on the monitoring plots, forest stands within the park are currently predominantly young or middle-aged (Table 1).

The quadratic mean diameter (QMD) of the plot was calculated for each plot. The quadratic mean diameter is the "average" diameter for the plot; specifically, the diameter of a hypothetical tree with its basal area equal to the plot's average basal area of live trees (Curtis and Marshall 2000). The plots are then classified into non-forested, pole, mature, and late-successional categories based on the following classification (adapted from Frelich and Lorimer 1991): non-forested = no trees in the plot; pole = $10 \text{ cm} \leq QMD > 26 \text{ cm}$; mature = $26 \text{ cm} \leq QMD > 46 \text{ cm}$; late-successional = $QMD \geq 46 \text{ cm}$ dbh. Table 1 shows the percentage of plots that fall into these categories.

Table 1. Distribution of plots in stand structural classes from 77 monitoring plots visited between 2007 and 2009 in the Delaware Water Gap National Recreation Area.

Stand structural class	Number of plots (n=77)	Percent of total plots
Non-forested	5	6%
Pole	40	52%
Mature	32	42%
Late-successional	0	0%

Forest Composition and Structure

The relative proportion of species among different strata of a forest stand provides information on the current and future composition of the forest. For this analysis, 36 plots in the xeric vegetation domain (dry, typically higher elevation forest types such as Dry Oak - Heath Forest and Dry Hemlock - Oak Forest) were analyzed. The relative basal area and density by species for trees, saplings, and seedlings are shown in Figure 3 (at the end of the Results section due to large image size). The charts in Figure 3 provide an illustration of how the species composition shifts among the canopy, sapling, and seedling layers of the forest.

Despite the dominance of oaks (*Quercus* spp.) in the canopy, oaks are underrepresented in the sapling layer, which is dominated by white pine (*Pinus strobus*), red maple (*Acer rubrum*), and black birch (*Betula lenta*). Oaks also make up a disproportionately smaller percentage of the seedling layer, which is predominantly maples (*Acer* spp.), shadbush (*Amelanchier arborea*), and black birch. If this trend continues, the park's dry forests will contain fewer oaks and more red maple, white pine, and black birch in the future. This failure of oak regeneration has been observed in xeric forests in other ERMN parks and throughout the Appalachian Mountains.

Forest Regeneration

One approach to assessing forest regeneration quantifies whether current seedling quantities are sufficient to restock a forest stand's canopy trees. McWilliams et al. (2005) developed an index for hardwood stands in Pennsylvania that assigns point values to seedlings by size class and to saplings observed within the 2-m radius circular microplots. McWilliams et al. (2005) suggested that the standard guideline for acceptable regeneration is an index value of 25 per microplot in areas with low deer densities. In areas where high deer densities are likely to impact tree regeneration an acceptable index value is 100. A forest plot is considered adequately regenerated if at least 70% of the microplots (three out of four microplots) exceed the stocking index (McWilliams et al. 2001).

Of the 72 forested plots assessed in DEWA, only 16 plots (21%) have adequate regeneration using the higher stocking index of 100. Using the lower stocking index of 25, approximately 57% (44 plots) of the forested plots have adequate regeneration. Compared to other ERMN parks, DEWA and Friendship Hill National Historic Site contain the lowest proportion of plots with sufficient regeneration. This regeneration failure could be due to one or more potentially interacting factors, including dense shade from canopy or subcanopy trees, competition from shrubs, ferns, or grasses, browse pressure, and/or soil infertility. In the future we hope to use the monitoring data to look for correlations between these factors and regeneration within the park.

Forest Health

Three exotic forest pests that are of concern in DEWA include gypsy moth (*Lymantria dispar*), hemlock woolly adelgid (*Adelges tsugae*), and elongate hemlock scale (*Fiorinia externa*). The presence of these insects is recorded at each tree within the monitoring plots. The percentage of trees on which these species were observed, the percent of plots in which these species were observed, and the average observed defoliation per tree are shown in Table 2.

Table 2. Percentage of trees on which key forest pest species were observed, the percentage of plots in which these species were observed, and the average observed percent defoliation per tree in monitoring plots (2007–2009) in Delaware Water Gap National Recreation Area.

Gypsy moth	Percent of trees	Percent of forest plots	Average percent defoliation per tree
2007	12%	43%	56%
2008	59%	88%	11%
2009	11%	33%	9%
Hemlock woolly adelgid	Percent of hemlock trees	Percent of hemlock plots	Average percent defoliation per tree
2007	10%	17%	1%
2008	28%	88%	17%
2009	2%	33%	0%
Elongate hemlock scale	Percent of hemlock trees	Percent of forest plots	Average percent defoliation per tree
2008	13%	38%	11%
2009	10%	67%	0%

Gypsy moth abundance peaked in 2008 with 88% of forested plots containing gypsy moth adults or caterpillars; however, average defoliation per tree declined through the three years. Defoliation was severe in many areas of the park in 2008; however, the ubiquitous nature of the gypsy moth caterpillars that year dilutes the average defoliation per tree.

The variability reported in the percentage of hemlock plots in which hemlock woolly adelgid and elongate hemlock scale were observed is probably a sampling artifact and not reflective of the distribution or abundance of these forest pests. Additional data are needed to determine if this monitoring program can provide accurate information on the spread of these two hemlock pests.

Snags

Standing dead trees, or snags, are important structural features in forests and provide habitat for cavity-nesting birds and mammals. The density and size of snags are indicative of habitat availability for those species.

Among the 72 forested plots, snags represent 8.1% of the total basal area (2.2 m^2/ha) and 6.1% of the total volume, on average. The average density of snags across the forested plots is 57.0 snags/ha, or 10.8% of total stem density. There is one snag for every 7.7 live trees, on average. For large snags, those with a DBH larger than 30 cm, the average density is 9.6 snags/ha, or 7.4% of total large stem density. There is one large snag for every 12.3 large live trees, on average. Comparatively, DEWA tends to have more large snags than found in other ERMN parks.

These values are typical of second-growth forests that are similar in age to those in DEWA. In a hemlock-northern hardwood stand in Pennsylvania standing snags accounted for 14% of the total basal area (6.7 m^2/ha) and 12% of the total stem density (49 snags/ha; Tritton and Siccama 1990). In mesic oak-hickory stands in Connecticut snags accounted for 5–15% of the total basal area (1.3–3.4 m^2/ha) and 8–19% of the total stem density (47–109 snags/ha; Tritton and Siccama 1990). In hardwood forests in West Virginia snag densities ranged from 22.4–55.1/ha (Carey 1983). In chestnut oak and oak-hickory stands in southwestern Virginia snag densities ranged from 62.2–69.2/ha (Rosenberg et al 1998).

Old-growth forests also exhibit variability in snag densities ranging from 10–20 snags/ha in southern Appalachia (Runkle 1998, 2000), to 43 snags/ha in Kentucky (McComb and Muller 1983), and 39–73 snag/ha in northern Michigan and Wisconsin (Goodburn and Lorimer 1998).

Coarse Woody Debris

Fallen logs, or coarse woody debris, provide important habitat for microbes, arthropods, amphibians, reptiles, small mammals, and fungi. Among the 72 forested plots in DEWA, the average coarse woody debris volume is 33.9 m^3/ha, which is 15.9% of the standing live tree volume on average. These values are typical of second-growth forests that are of similar age to those in DEWA.

Coarse woody debris volume can range from 25 m^3/ha in even-aged northern hardwood stands to 102 m^3/ha in old-growth northern hardwood forests in northern Michigan and Wisconsin (Goodburn and Lorimer 1998). Other published values include 46–132 m^3/ha for mixed oak forests (Harmon et al 1983) and 48 m^3/ha for old-growth forests in eastern Kentucky (Muller and Liu 1991), though the latter study only measured logs >20 cm in diameter.

Shrubs

The composition of the shrub layer varies between xeric (dry) and mesic (moist) habitats in the park (Table 3). Microplots in xeric sites contain three species on average, typically native ericaceous species such as blueberries (*Vaccinium* spp.), huckleberries (*Gaylussacia* spp.), or laurels (*Kalmia* spp.). Microplots in mesic sites contain 2.5 species on average, typically exotic invasive species such as multiflora rose (*Rosa multiflora*) and Japanese barberry (*Berberis thunbergii*).

Groundstory Diversity and Nativity

The groundstory of most vegetation communities is the most diverse strata. Thus, diversity and nativity of this vegetation layer is an important component of the overall health of the vegetation community. Table 4 shows several metrics that will be monitored to determine trends in groundstory vegetation diversity and nativity in DEWA. As would be expected, the percent cover and species richness of nonnative plant species is much higher in the mesic plots than in the xeric plots, as is the overall plot and quadrat species richness.

Deer Browse Indicators

Data on numerous herbaceous plant species that are considered sensitive to deer browse are being collected. The two most abundant of these species have the best potential to serve as indicators for long-term monitoring. Jack-in-the-pulpit (*Ariseama triphyllum*) occurred in 32% of the plots with an average quadrat frequency of 41%; this species will likely be a good indicator in mesic habitats. Canada mayflower (*Maianthemum canadense*), occurring in 30% of the plots with an average quadrat frequency of 32%, will likely be a good indicator in drier habitats. Canada mayflower is also being considered as a deer browse indicator species in state forest lands in Pennsylvania (Diefenbach and Fritsky 2007). The number of reproducing, non-reproducing, browsed, and non-browsed plants in each quadrat is collected, along with the height of the three tallest plants in each quadrat. We will be looking for changes in these variables through time to gauge the survival and persistence of these species.

Habitat Diversity

Biotic homogenization is the process by which regional biodiversity declines through time due to the addition of widespread exotic species as well as the loss of native species (Olden and Rooney 2006). Homogenization occurs when the variety of different vegetation types within a park become more similar to each other, shifting from specialized, unique vegetation communities towards a more generic, homogeneous species composition throughout. Biotic homogenization can be caused by many factors, including land use change, climate change, deer browse, soil fertility, and invasive exotic animal and plant species.

Jaccard's similarity index can be used to evaluate biotic homogenization by comparing the similarity between the species composition of any two plots. The average Jaccard's index for the park includes all possible between-plot comparisons and provides a measure of the diversity of habitats in the park. The average Jaccard's index for DEWA's monitoring plots is 0.148.

Table 3. Average percent cover and number of stems per microplot for the most abundant shrub species in xeric and mesic plots in the Delaware Water Gap National Recreation Area.

Shrub species	Percent cover	Number of stems
Xeric Plots (n=37)		
Black huckleberry (*Gaylussacia baccata*)	14.5%	23.8
Lowbush blueberry (*Vaccinium angustifolium*)	9.3%	22.9
Blue Ridge blueberry (*Vaccinium pallidum*)	6.1%	12.9
Deerberry (*Vaccinium stamineum*)	3.7%	6.2
Mountain laurel (*Kalmia latifolia*)	3.6%	1.0
Scrub oak (*Quercus ilicifolia*)	2.6%	1.3
Eastern teaberry (*Gaultheria procumbens*)	2.0%	12.9
Sheep laurel (*Kalmia angustifolia*)	1.2%	4.2
Mesic Plots (n=40)		
Multiflora rose (*Rosa multiflora*)	9.2%	4.2
Spicebush (*Lindera benzoin*)	5.2%	2.3
Japanese barberry (*Berberis thunbergii*)	3.9%	3.1
Autumn olive (*Elaeagnus umbellata*)	3.3%	0.2
Gray dogwood (*Cornus racemosa*)	2.5%	1.6
Morrow's honeysuckle (*Lonicera morrowii*)	2.4%	0.4

Table 4. Average values for several groundstory diversity measures, calculated from monitoring plot data in the Delaware Water Gap National Recreation Area.

Diversity measure	Xeric plots (n=37)	Mesic plots (n=40)
Plot richness (from all quadrats within a plot)	16.4	32.1
Quadrat Richness	4.2	8.5
Percent of total quadrat cover from nonnative species	1.1%	31.1%
Percent of total quadrat cover from native species	94.6%	64.3%
Percent of quadrat richness from nonnative species	1.4%	21.8%
Percent of quadrat richness from native species	93.7%	70.3%

Tracking the change in Jaccard's index through time will provide information on the extent and magnitude of biotic homogenization within the park. Through time, an increase in the average Jaccard's index would indicate that the park's vegetation types are becoming less diverse.

Overall, 516 taxa of plants were observed in the vegetation montoring plots between 2007 and 2009. A list of these taxa is provided in the Appendix.

Invasive Exotic Plant Species

Twenty-seven invasive exotic plant species were observed in the monitoring plots (Table 5) between 2007 and 2009. Only 39% of the plots were free of invasive plant species, while 43% of the plots contained three or more invasive plant species. The most commonly observed invasive exotic plant species were Japanese barberry (*Berberis thunbergii*) in 36 plots, Japanese stiltgrass (*Microstegium vimineum*) in 32 plots, garlic mustard (*Alliaria petiolata*) in 30 plots, and multiflora rose (*Rosa multiflora*) in 30 plots.

Early Detection of Exotic Invasive Plants and Animals

No species from the early detection terrestrial plant and forest pest/pathogen watch lists were observed in DEWA in 2007.

Three occurrences of narrowleaf bittercress (*Cardamine impatiens*) were documented between 2008 and 2009. Narrowleaf bittercress was observed in the floodplain off of Peters Canoe Camp Road in Sussex County, New Jersey in 2008; the vegetation monitoring field crew removed and disposed of all of the plants at this site. In 2009, narrowleaf bittercress was found by the vegetation monitoring field crew at two additional locations: 1) in a plantation between Route 209 and the Delaware River in Pike County, Pennsylvnia; and 2) between the Delaware River and Old Mine Road, north of mile marker #22, in Sussex County, New Jersey. In both locations there were too many plants for the crew to remove during their field visits. The detection of three occurrences of this species over the past two years suggests that it likely will be a significant invader along the Delaware River floodplain and possibly in other moist habitats within the park over the next few years.

Severe dieback on native viburnum shrubs (*Viburnum* spp.) was observed at three monitoring plots in the Flat Brook valley in the New Jersey portion of the park in 2009. Although conclusive evidence of the viburnum leaf beetle (*Pyrrhalta viburni*) was not observed, it was assumed that viburnum leaf beetles were responsible, since no other shrub species in the areas showed evidence of decline. Based on these observations, it is likely that viburnum leaf beetle is wide-spread in the Flatbrook valley and causing significant dieback in the native viburnum shrubs there.

The locations of these new exotic invasive species were reported to park natural resource managers in accordance with the ERMN Invasive Species Early Detection and Rapid Response protocol (Keefer et al. 2009).

Table 5. Invasive exotic plant species observed in monitoring plots in the Delaware Water Gap National Recreation Area between 2007–2009.

Common name	Scientific name	Observed in number of plots (n=77)
Japanese barberry	*Berberis thunbergii*	36
Japanese stiltgrass	*Microstegium vimineum*	32
garlic mustard	*Alliaria petiolata*	30
multiflora rose	*Rosa multiflora*	30
Oriental bittersweer	*Celastrus orbiculatus*	22
Morrow's honeysuckle	*Lonicera morrowii*	18
Oriental lady's thumb	*Polygonum caespitosum*	17
autumn olive	*Elaeagnus umbellata*	13
privet	*Ligustrum* spp.	6
ground ivy	*Glechoma hederacea*	5
burning bush	*Euonymus alatus*	5
tree of heaven	*Ailanthus altissima*	4
dame's rocket	*Hesperis matronalis*	4
purple loosestrife	*Lythrum salicaria*	4
Japanese knotweed	*Polygonum cuspidatum*	4
wine raspberry	*Rubus phoenicolasius*	4
Japanese honeysuckle	*Lonicera japonica*	3
Amur honeysuckle	*Lonicera maackii*	3
Norway maple	*Acer platanoides*	1
wild chervil	*Anthriscus sylvestris*	1
narrowleaf bittercress	*Cardamine impatiens*	1
Canada thistle	*Cirsium arvense*	1
star-mustard	*Coincya monensis*	1
Russian olive	*Elaeagnus angustifolia*	1
sericea lespedeza	*Lespedeza cuneata*	1
common mullein	*Verbascum thapsus*	1
spotted knapweed	*Centaurea stoebe* ssp. *micranthos*	1

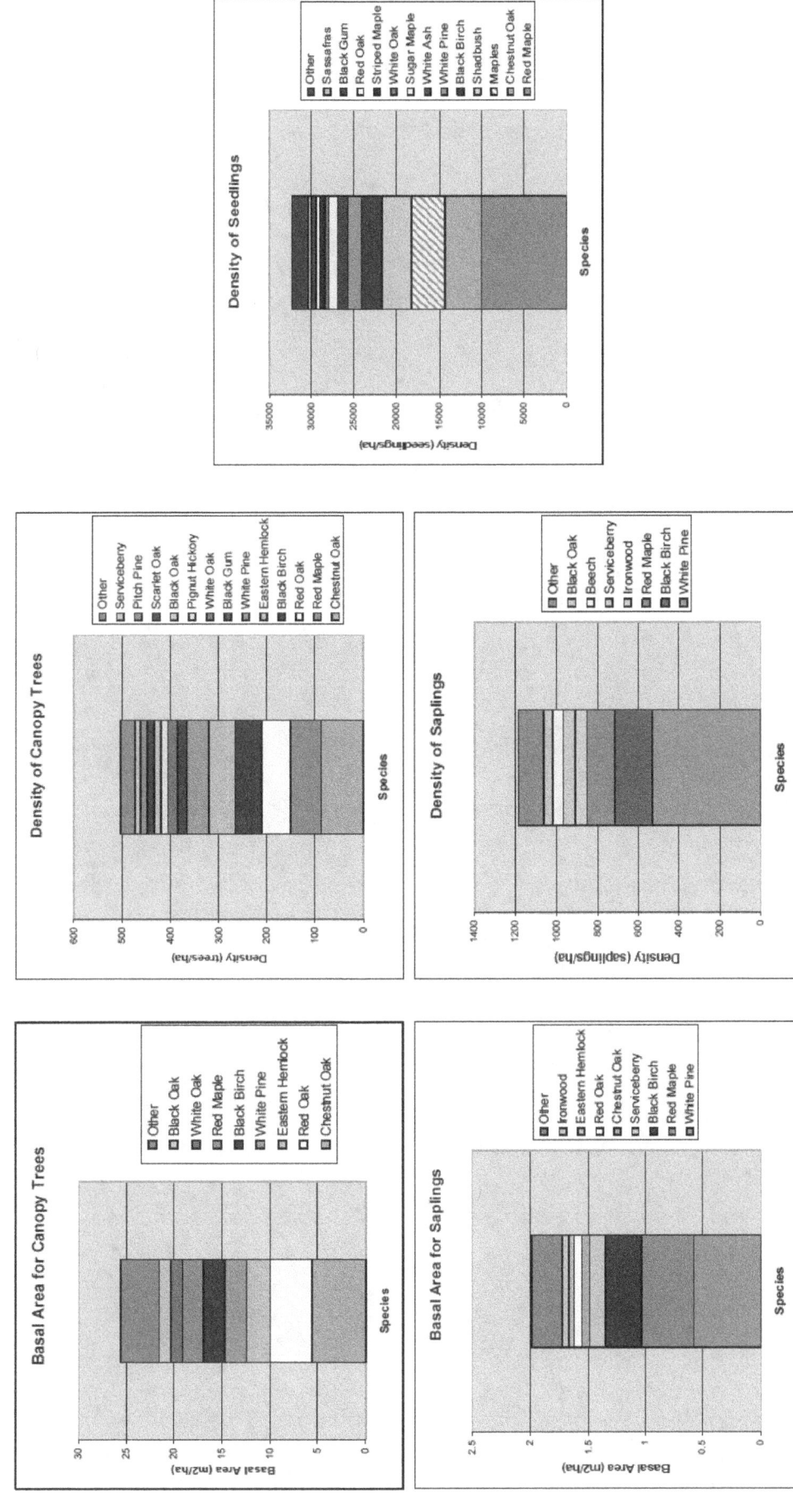

Figure 3. Basal area and density of species for canopy trees (top row), saplings (bottom row), and seedlings (right-most image) in the xeric plots (n=36) in the Delaware Water Gap National Recreation Area. These charts provide an illustration of the composition of various strata in the park's dry forest types. The color code for each species is the same in all charts.

15

Discussion

This report summarized the vegetation monitoring data collected between 2007 and 2009 in the Delaware Water Gap National Recreation Area and presented the condition of the park's vegetation, as compared to expected ranges of variability for eastern forest systems. In general, forests in DEWA are typical of other second-growth forests in the Appalachian Mountains. However, results from the monitoring data underscore two important points for park managers: 1) invasive exotic plant species are a pervasive and spreading threat to the park's resources; and 2) factors contributing to poor tree regeneration, particularly of oaks, need to be investigated further in order to evaluate potential management actions.

That invasive exotic plant species are a serious and growing threat to park resources is not a novel assertion. The monitoring data concur with previous research in the park documenting that invasive exotic species are most abundant in mesic and riparian areas, especially in successional areas that were formerly agricultural or recently disturbed (Eichelberger and Perles 2009). These findings underscore the vital importance of the many ongoing projects in DEWA directed by park managers, external researchers, and the Exotic Pest Management Teams that are addressing invasive exotic plants. When possible, additional resources should be strategically allocated to managing invasive exotic species through the following actions:

a) Manage invasive exotic plants in sensitive, rare habitats.
b) Detect and eliminate (when possible) new populations of invasive exotic species novel to the park (implementation of the Early Detection and Rapid Response protocol).
c) Work with partners to acquire and release approved biological controls for invasive exotic species that are widespread and abundant in the park.

Poor tree regeneration, especially in oak species (*Quercus* spp.), has been documented widely in Pennsylvania and the surrounding areas. This regeneration failure could be attributed to one or more of the following factors: dense shade from canopy or subcanopy trees; competition from shrubs, ferns, or grasses; altered disturbance regimes, including fire suppression; browse pressure from white-tailed deer; and/or soil infertility. Most forest stands in the park are closed-canopy with few canopy gaps that are critical for oak regeneration. Without the periodic surface fires and occasional canopy gaps that perpetuated oak forests in previous centuries (Brose et al 2008), oak seedlings are at a competitive disadvantage to other tree species (Abrams 1998). Stands with ideal conditions for oak regeneration contain less than 70% stocking of the canopy and less than 70% cover in the groundstory of competing vegetation such as shrubs, ferns, and grasses (Brose et al 2008). Many of the young and middle-aged forest stands in DEWA may not meet these requirements for regeneration simply due to their age.

In addition, changes in land use and land management over the previous decades have led to expanded native white-tailed deer populations (Latham et al. 2005). Selective browsing by deer leads to altered species composition towards dominance of non-preferred and browse-resilient tree species such as maples (*Acer* spp.) and birches (*Betula* spp.), along with overall reduced survival of tree seedlings and saplings, especially of browse-preferred species such as oaks (Russell et al. 2001, Horsley et al. 2003, Latham et al. 2005). Another confounding factor for some tree species may be soil infertility. Acid deposition can have significant effects on soils, including depletion of base cations such as calcium and magnesium, and the mobilization of aluminum and manganese (Driscoll et al. 2001). These changes in soil chemistry have been linked to decreases in sugar maple (*Acer saccharum*) seedlings and increases in hay-scented fern (*Dennstaedtia punctilobula*) cover, which generally inhibits seedling growth (Sharpe and Halofsky 2004).

As more data on both vegetation and soil are collected from the monitoring plots we will investigate correlations between the factors discussed above and tree regeneration in DEWA. We hope to be able to provide guidance on potential management actions (including "let the forest grow old") pertaining to forest regeneration.

Literature Cited

Abrams, M. 1998. The red maple paradox. BioScience 48(5):355–364.

Brose, P. H., K. W. Gottschalk, S. B. Horsley, P. D. Knopp, J. N. Kochenderfer, B. J. McGuinness, G. W. Miller, T. E. Ristau, S. H. Stoleson, and S. L. Stout. 2008. Prescribing regeneration treatments for mixed-oak forests in the Mid-Atlantic region. Gen. Tech. Rep. NRS-33. Newtown Square, PA. U.S. Department of Agriculture, Forest Service, Northern Research Station.

Carey, A. B. 1983. Cavities in trees in hardwood forests. Pp 167–184. *In* Snag habitat management: Proc. Symp., Davis, J. W., G. A. Goodwin, and R. A. Ockenfels, Technical Coordinators. USDA Forest Service General Technical Report. RM-99.

Comiskey, J. A., J. P. Schmit, and G. Tierney. 2009. Mid-Atlantic Network forest vegetation monitoring protocol. Natural Resource Report NPS/MIDN/NRR—2009/119. National Park Service, Fort Collins, CO.

Curtis, R. O., and D. D. Marshall. 2000. Why quadratic mean diameter? Western Journal of Applied Forestry. 15(3):137–139.

Diefenbach, D. R., and R. S. Fritsky. 2007. Developing and testing a rapid assessment protocol for monitoring vegetation changes on state forest lands. Final Report submitted to the Department of Conservation and Natural Resources, PA.

Driscoll, C. T., G. B. Lawrence, A. J. Bulger, T. J. Butler, C. S. Cronan, C. Eagar, K. F. Lambert, G. E. Likens, J. L. Stoddard, and K. C. Weathers. 2001. Acidic deposition in the northeastern United States: sources and inputs, ecosystem effects, and management strategies. BioScience 51(3):180–198.

Eichelberger, B. A., and S. J. Perles. 2009. Determining the status and trends of key invasive plant species in the Delaware Water Gap National Recreation Area. Technical Report NPS/NER/NRTR—2009/134. National Park Service. Philadelphia, PA.

Fancy, S. G., J. E. Gross, and S. L. Carter. 2009. Monitoring the condition of natural resources in U.S. national parks. Environmental Monitoring and Assessment 151:161–174.

Frelich, L. E., and C. G. Lorimer. 1991. Natural disturbance regimes in hemlock-hardwood forests of the upper Great Lakes region. Ecological Monographs 61:145–164

Goodburn, J. M., and C. G. Lorimer. 1998. Cavity trees and coarse woody debris in old-growth and managed northern hardwood forests in Wisconsin and Michigan. Canadian Journal of Forest Research 28:427–438.

Keefer, J. S., M. R. Marshall, and B. R. Mitchell. 2009. Early detection of invasive species— surveillance and rapid response for the Eastern Rivers and Mountains and Northeast Temperate networks. Natural Resource Report NPS/ERMN/NRR—2009/XXX. National Park Service, Fort Collins, CO.

Harmon, M. E., J. F. Franklin, F. J. Swanson, P. Sollins, S. V. Gregory, J. D. Lattin, N. H. Anderson, S. P. Cline, N. G. Aumen, J. R. Sedell, S. W. Liekaemper, D. Cromack, Jr., and K. W. Cumins. 1983. Ecology of coarse woody debris in temperate ecosystems. Advances in Ecological Research 15:133–302.

Horsely, S. B., S. L. Stout, and D. S. DeCalesta. 2003. White-tailed deer impact on the vegetation dynamics of a northern hardwood forest. Ecological Applications 13(1):98–118.

Latham, R. E., J. Beyea, M. Benner, C. A. Dunn, M. A. Fajvan, R. R. Freed, M. Grund, S. B. Horsley, A. F. Rhoads, and B. P. Shissler. 2005. Managing white-tailed deer in forest habitat from an ecosystem perspective: Pennsylvania case study. Report by the Deer Management Forum for Audubon Pennsylvania and Pennsylvania Habitat Alliance. Harrisburg, PA.

Marshall, M. R., and N. B. Piekielek. 2007. Eastern Rivers and Mountains Network Ecological Monitoring Plan. Natural Resource Report NPS/ERMN/NRR—2007/017. National Park Service. Fort Collins, CO.

McComb, W. C., and R. N. Muller. 1983. Snag densities in old-growth and second-growth Appalachian forests. The Journal of Wildlife Management 47(2):376–382.

McDonald, T. L. 2004. GRTS for the Average Joe: A GRTS Sampler for Windows. Online http://www.west-inc.com/biometrics_reports.php.

McWilliams, W. H., S. L. King, and C. T. Scott. 2001. Assessing regeneration adequacy in Pennsylvania's forests: a pilot study. In Reams, G. L., R. E. McRoberts, P. C. Van Deusen, eds. Proceedings, 2nd Annual Forest Inventory and Analysis symposium, 2000 October 17–18, Salt Lake City, UT. Gen. Tech. Rep. SRS-47. Asheville, NC. U.S. Department of Agriculture, Forest Service, Southern Research Station 119–122.

McWilliams, W. H., T. W. Bowersox, P. H. Brose, D. A. Devlin, J. C. Finley, K. W. Gottschalk, S. Horsley, S. L. King, B. M. LaPoint, T. W. Lister, L. H. McCormick, G. W. Miller, C. T. Scott, H. Steele, K. C. Steiner, S. L. Stout, J. A.Westfall, and R. L. White. 2005. Measuring tree seedlings and associated understory vegetation in Pennsylvania's forests. In: McRoberts, R. E., G. A. Reams, P. C. Van Deusen, and W. H. McWilliams. Cieszewski, Chris J., eds. 2005. Proceedings of the Fourth Annual Forest Inventory and Analysis Symposium; 2002 November 19–21; New Orleans, LA. Gen. Tech. Rep. NC-252. St. Paul, MN: U.S. Department of Agriculture, Forest Service, North Central Research Station.

Muller, R. N. and Y. Liu. 1991. Coarse woody debris in an old-growth deciduous forest on the Cumberland Plateau, southeastern Kentucky. Canadian Journal of Forest Research. 21:1567–1572.

Olden, J. D., and T. P. Rooney. 2006. On defining and quantifying biotic homogenization. Global Ecology and Biogeography 15(2):113–120.

Perles, S., J. Finley, and M. Marshall. 2009. Vegetation Monitoring Protocol for the Eastern Rivers and Mountains Network, Version 1. Natural Resource Report NPS/ERMN/NRR—2009/DRAFT. National Park Service. Fort Collins, CO.

Rentch, J. S. 2006. Structure and functioning of terrestrial ecosystems in the Eastern Rivers and Mountains Network: Conceptual Models and Vital Signs Monitoring. Natural Resources Report NPS/NER/NRR—2006/007. National Park Service. Philadelphia, PA.

Rosenberg, D. K., J. D. Fraser, and D. F. Stauffer. 1988. Use and characteristics of snags in young and old forest stands in southwest Virginia. Forest Science. 34(1):224–228.

Runkle, J. R. 1998. Changes in Southern Appalachian canopy tree gaps sampled thrice. Ecology 79(5):1768–1780.

Runkle, J. R. 2000. Canopy tree turnover in old-growth mesic forests in eastern North America. Ecology 81(2):554–567.

Russell, F. L, D. B. Zippin, and N. L. Fowler. 2001. Effects of white-tailed deer (*Odocoileus virginianus*) on plants, plant populations, and communities: a review. American Midland Naturalist 146(1)1–26.

Sanders, S., S. E. Johnson, and D. M. Waller. 2006. General vegetation monitoring protocol for the Great Lakes Network, Version 1.0. National Park Service, Great Lakes Network, Ashland, WI.

Schmit, J. P., D. C. Chojnacky, and M. Milton. 2006. Forest Monitoring Protocol, Version 1.0. National Park Service. National Capital Region Network. Washington, DC.

Sharpe, W. E., and J. E. Halofsky. 2004. Hay-scented fern (*Dennstaedtia punctilobula*) and sugar maple (Acer saccharum) seedling occurrence with varying soil acidity in Pennsylvania. Proceedings of the 14th Central Hardwood Forest Conference: 2004 March 16–19; Wooster, OH. Gen. Tech. Rep. NE-316. U.S. Department of Agriculture, Forest Service, Northeastern Research Station. Pp. 265–270.

Stevens, D. L., and A. N. Olsen. 2004. Spatially balanced sampling of natural resources. Journal of American Statistical Association 99(465):262–278.

Tierney, G., and D. Faber-Langendoen. 2007. NPS Northeast Temperate Network Long-term Forest Monitoring Protocol. Natural Resources Report NPS/NETN/NRR—XXXX/XXX. National Park Service. Fort Collins, CO.

Tierney, G. L., D. Faber-Langendoen, B. R. Mitchell, W. G. Shriver, and J. P. Gibbs. 2009. Monitoring and evaluating the ecological integrity of forest ecosystems. Frontiers in Ecology and the Environment 7, doi:10.1890/070176

Tritton, L. M., and T. G. Siccama. 1990. What proportion of standing trees in forests of the Northeast are dead? Bulletin of the Torrey Botanical Club 117:163–166.

United States Department of Agriculture (USDA), Natural Resource Conservation Service (NRCS). 2007. The PLANTS Database (http://plants.usda.gov). National Plant Data Center, Baton Rouge, LA 70874-4490 USA.

United States Forest Service (USFS). 2007. Forest Inventory and Analysis National Core Field Guide. Version 4.0. United States Forest Service.

Van Wagner, C. E. 1964. The line-intersect method in forest fuel sampling. Forest Science 28:267–276.

Appendix. Plants observed in Delaware Water Gap National Recreation Area during vegetation monitoring plot sampling, 2007–2009.

Nomenclature follows the Master Plant List in the Vegetation and Soil Monitoring Database (Perles et al 2009), which is based on the USDA PLANTS Database (USDA, NRCS 2007).

Family	Latin name	Common name
Aceraceae	*Acer negundo*	boxelder
	Acer pensylvanicum	striped maple
	Acer platanoides	Norway maple
	Acer rubrum	red maple
	Acer saccharinum	silver maple
	Acer saccharum	sugar maple
	Acer sp.	maple
Anacardiaceae	*Rhus typhina*	staghorn sumac
	Toxicodendron radicans	eastern poison ivy
Apiaceae	*Angelica atropurpurea*	purplestem angelica
	Anthriscus sylvestris	wild chervil
	Cryptotaenia canadensis	Canadian honewort
	Daucus carota	Queen Anne's lace
	Hydrocotyle americana	American marshpennywort
	Osmorhiza claytonii	Clayton's sweetroot
	Osmorhiza longistylis	longstyle sweetroot
	Osmorhiza sp.	sweetroot
	Sanicula canadensis var. canadensis	Canadian blacksnakeroot
	Sanicula sp.	sanicle
	Zizia aurea	golden zizia
Apocynaceae	*Apocynum androsaemifolium*	spreading dogbane
	Apocynum sp.	dogbane
Aquifoliaceae	*Ilex Montana*	mountain holly
	Ilex sp.	holly
	Ilex verticillata	common winterberry
Araceae	*Arisaema dracontium*	green dragon
	Arisaema triphyllum	Jack in the pulpit
	Symplocarpus foetidus	skunk cabbage
Araliaceae	*Aralia nudicaulis*	wild sarsaparilla
Aristolochiaceae	*Aristolochia serpentaria*	Virginia snakeroot
Asclepiadaceae	*Asclepias incarnata*	swamp milkweed
	Asclepias sp.	milkweed
	Asclepias syriaca	common milkweed
Aspleniaceae	*Asplenium platyneuron*	ebony spleenwort
Asteraceae	*Achillea millefolium*	common yarrow
	Ageratina altissima	white snakeroot
	Ambrosia artemisiifolia	annual ragweed
	Antennaria howellii	Howell's pussytoes
	Antennaria plantaginifolia	woman's tobacco
	Antennaria sp.	pussytoes
	Aster sp.	aster
	Bidens sp.	beggarticks
	Centaurea stoebe ssp. micranthos	spotted knapweed
	Cirsium arvense	Canada thistle
	Cirsium discolor	field thistle
	Cirsium sp.	thistle
	Erechtites hieraciifolia	American burnweed
	Erigeron strigosus	prairie fleabane
	Eupatorium perfoliatum	common boneset
	Eupatorium sp.	thoroughwort
	Eurybia divaricata	white wood aster
	Euthamia graminifolia	flat-top goldentop
	Hieracium ×flagellare	hawkweed

Family	Latin name	Common name
Asteraceae (cont)	*Hieracium caespitosum*	meadow hawkweed
	Hieracium piloselloides	tall hawkweed
	Hieracium scabrum	rough hawkweed
	Hieracium sp.	hawkweed
	Hieracium venosum	rattlesnakeweed
	Krigia biflora	twoflower dwarfdandelion
	Leucanthemum vulgare	oxeye daisy
	Prenanthes sp.	rattlesnakeroot
	Rudbeckia hirta	blackeyed Susan
	Rudbeckia sp.	coneflower
	Solidago altissima	late goldenrod
	Solidago caesia	wreath goldenrod
	Solidago flexicaulis	zigzag goldenrod
	Solidago gigantea	giant goldenrod
	Solidago juncea	early goldenrod
	Solidago rugosa	wrinkleleaf goldenrod
	Solidago sp.	goldenrod
	Symphyotrichum lanceolatum	white panicle aster
	Symphyotrichum prenanthoides	crookedstem aster
	Taraxacum officinale	common dandelion
	Taraxacum sp.	dandelion
Balsaminaceae	*Impatiens capensis*	jewelweed
	Impatiens sp.	touch-me-not
Berberidaceae	*Berberis thunbergii*	Japanese barberry
	Caulophyllum thalictroides	blue cohosh
	Podophyllum peltatum	mayapple
Betulaceae	*Alnus incana*	gray alder
	Betula alleghaniensis	yellow birch
	Betula lenta	sweet birch
	Betula nigra	river birch
	Betula populifolia	gray birch
	Carpinus caroliniana	American hornbeam
	Corylus americana	American hazelnut
	Ostrya virginiana	hophornbeam
Boraginaceae	*Cynoglossum virginianum*	wild comfrey
	Hackelia virginiana	beggarslice
Brassicaceae	*Alliaria petiolata*	garlic mustard
	Arabis glabra	tower rockcress
	Arabis laevigata	smooth rockcress
	Arabis lyrata	lyrate rockcress
	Barbarea vulgaris	garden yellowrocket
	Cardamine diphylla	crinkleroot
	Cardamine impatiens	narrowleaf bittercress
	Cardamine sp.	bittercress
	Coincya monensis	star-mustard
	Hesperis matronalis	dames rocket
	Lepidium sp.	pepperweed
	Nasturtium officinale	watercress
Campanulaceae	*Lobelia inflata*	Indian-tobacco
	Triodanis perfoliata	clasping Venus' looking-glass
Caprifoliaceae	*Lonicera* ×*bella*	showy fly honeysuckle
	Lonicera japonica	Japanese honeysuckle
	Lonicera maackii	Amur honeysuckle
	Lonicera morrowii	Morrow's honeysuckle
	Lonicera sp.	honeysuckle
	Sambucus sp.	elderberry
	Viburnum acerifolium	mapleleaf viburnum
	Viburnum dentatum	southern arrowwood
	Viburnum lentago	nannyberry
	Viburnum nudum var. *cassinoides*	withe-rod
	Viburnum prunifolium	blackhaw

Family	Latin name	Common name
Caprifoliaceae (cont)	*Viburnum recognitum*	northern arrowwood
	Viburnum sp.	viburnum
Caryophyllaceae	*Cerastium fontanum*	common mouse-ear chickweed
	Dianthus armeria	Deptford pink
	Dianthus sp.	pink
	Myosoton aquaticum	giantchickweed
	Paronychia canadensis	smooth forked nailwort
	Saponaria officinalis	bouncingbet
	Stellaria graminea	grasslike starwort
	Stellaria longifolia	longleaf starwort
	Stellaria media	common chickweed
Celastraceae	*Celastrus orbiculatus*	Oriental bittersweet
	Euonymus alatus	burningbush
	Euonymus americanus	bursting-heart
	Euonymus atropurpureus	burningbush
Chenopodiaceae	*Chenopodium album*	lambsquarters
	Chenopodium sp.	goosefoot
Clethraceae	*Clethra alnifolia*	coastal sweetpepperbush
Clusiaceae	*Hypericum perforatum*	common St. Johnswort
	Hypericum punctatum	spotted St. Johnswort
Commelinaceae	*Commelina communis*	Asiatic dayflower
	Commelina sp.	dayflower
Convolvulaceae	*Convolvulus arvensis*	field bindweed
Cornaceae	*Cornus alternifolia*	alternateleaf dogwood
	Cornus amomum	silky dogwood
	Cornus florida	flowering dogwood
	Cornus racemosa	gray dogwood
	Cornus sp.	dogwood
	Nyssa sylvatica	blackgum
Crassulaceae	*Sedum sarmentosum*	stringy stonecrop
Cucurbitaceae	*Echinocystis lobata*	wild cucumber
Cupressaceae	*Juniperus virginiana*	eastern redcedar
Cuscutaceae	*Cuscuta gronovii*	scaldweed
Cyperaceae	*Carex abscondita*	thicket sedge
	Carex amphibola	eastern narrowleaf sedge
	Carex appalachica	Appalachian sedge
	Carex arctata	drooping woodland sedge
	Carex argyrantha	hay sedge
	Carex blanda	eastern woodland sedge
	Carex bromoides	bromelike sedge
	Carex cephaloidea	thinleaf sedge
	Carex cephalophora	oval-leaf sedge
	Carex crinita	fringed sedge
	Carex debilis var. *debilis*	white edge sedge
	Carex debilis var. *rudgei*	white edge sedge
	Carex deweyana	Dewey sedge
	Carex digitalis	slender woodland sedge
	Carex gracillima	graceful sedge
	Carex granularis	limestone meadow sedge
	Carex grayi	Gray's sedge
	Carex gynandra	nodding sedge
	Carex hirtifolia	pubescent sedge
	Carex intumescens	greater bladder sedge
	Carex laevivaginata	smoothsheath sedge
	Carex laxiculmis	spreading sedge
	Carex laxiculmis var. *laxiculmis*	spreading sedge
	Carex laxiflora	broad looseflower sedge
	Carex leavenworthii	Leavenworth's sedge
	Carex lucorum	Blue Ridge sedge
	Carex lurida	shallow sedge
	Carex molesta	troublesome sedge

Family	Latin name	Common name
Cyperaceae (cont)	*Carex oligocarpa*	richwoods sedge
	Carex pensylvanica	Pennsylvania sedge
	Carex prasina	drooping sedge
	Carex radiate	eastern star sedge
	Carex rosea	rosy sedge
	Carex scoparia	broom sedge
	Carex sp.	sedge
	Carex sparganioides	burr reed sedge
	Carex sprengelii	Sprengel's sedge
	Carex stipata	owlfruit sedge
	Carex stipata var. *stipata*	owlfruit sedge
	Carex stricta	upright sedge
	Carex swanii	Swan's sedge
	Carex tenera	quill sedge
	Carex tribuloides	blunt broom sedge
	Carex trichocarpa	hairyfruit sedge
	Carex virescens	ribbed sedge
	Carex vulpinoidea	fox sedge
	Carex willdenowii	Willdenow's sedge
	Scirpus expansus	woodland bulrush
	Scirpus sp.	bulrush
	Trichophorum planifolium	bashful bulrush
Dennstaedtiaceae	*Dennstaedtia punctilobula*	eastern hayscented fern
	Pteridium aquilinum	western brackenfern
Dioscoreaceae	*Dioscorea quaternata*	fourleaf yam
	Dioscorea sp.	yam
	Dioscorea villosa	wild yam
Dryopteridaceae	*Athyrium filix-femina*	common ladyfern
	Athyrium filix-femina ssp. *angustum*	subarctic ladyfern
	Cystopteris bulbifera	bulblet bladderfern
	Cystopteris tenuis	upland brittle bladderfern
	Deparia acrostichoides	silver false spleenwort
	Dryopteris carthusiana	spinulose woodfern
	Dryopteris cristata	crested woodfern
	Dryopteris intermedia	intermediate woodfern
	Dryopteris marginalis	marginal woodfern
	Dryopteris sp.	woodfern
	Matteuccia struthiopteris	ostrich fern
	Onoclea sensibilis	sensitive fern
	Polystichum acrostichoides	Christmas fern
Elaeagnaceae	*Elaeagnus angustifolia*	Russian olive
	Elaeagnus umbellata	autumn olive
Equisetaceae	*Equisetum arvense*	field horsetail
Ericaceae	*Epigaea repens*	trailing arbutus
	Gaultheria procumbens	eastern teaberry
	Gaylussacia baccata	black huckleberry
	Kalmia angustifolia	sheep laurel
	Kalmia latifolia	mountain laurel
	Lyonia ligustrina	maleberry
	Rhododendron maximum	great laurel
	Rhododendron prinophyllum	early azalea
	Rhododendron sp.	rhododendron
	Vaccinium angustifolium	lowbush blueberry
	Vaccinium corymbosum	highbush blueberry
	Vaccinium pallidum	Blue Ridge blueberry
	Vaccinium stamineum	deerberry
Euphorbiaceae	*Acalypha rhomboidea*	common threeseed mercury
	Chamaesyce maculata	spotted sandmat
	Euphorbia cyparissias	cypress spurge
Fabaceae	*Amphicarpaea bracteata*	American hogpeanut
	Baptisia tinctoria	horseflyweed

Family	Latin name	Common name
Fabaceae (cont)	*Desmodium glutinosum*	pointedleaf ticktrefoil
	Desmodium sp.	ticktrefoil
	Gleditsia triacanthos	honeylocust
	Lespedeza cuneata	sericea lespedeza
	Lespedeza sp.	lespedeza
	Melilotus officinalis	yellow sweetclover
	Melilotus sp.	sweetclover
	Robinia pseudoacacia	black locust
	Tephrosia sp.	hoarypea
	Trifolium pratense	red clover
Fagaceae	*Castanea dentata*	American chestnut
	Fagus grandifolia	American beech
	Quercus alba	white oak
	Quercus bicolor	swamp white oak
	Quercus coccinea	scarlet oak
	Quercus ilicifolia	scrub oak
	Quercus prinus	chestnut oak
	Quercus rubra	northern red oak
	Quercus sp.	oak
	Quercus velutina	black oak
Geraniaceae	*Geranium maculatum*	spotted geranium
Grossulariaceae	*Ribes* sp.	currant
Hamamelidaceae	*Hamamelis virginiana*	American witchhazel
Iridaceae	*Iris* sp.	iris
	Sisyrinchium angustifolium	narrowleaf blue-eyed grass
Juglandaceae	*Carya alba*	mockernut hickory
	Carya cordiformis	bitternut hickory
	Carya glabra	pignut hickory
	Carya ovata	shagbark hickory
	Carya sp.	hickory
	Juglans nigra	black walnut
Juncaceae	*Juncus effusus*	common rush
	Juncus sp.	rush
	Juncus tenuis	poverty rush
	Luzula multiflora	common woodrush
Lamiaceae	*Agastache scrophulariifolia*	purple giant hyssop
	Clinopodium vulgare	wild basil
	Collinsonia canadensis	richweed
	Cunila origanoides	common dittany
	Glechoma hederacea	ground ivy
	Leonurus cardiaca	common motherwort
	Lycopus sp.	waterhorehound
	Mentha ×piperita	peppermint
	Monarda fistulosa	wild bergamot
	Prunella vulgaris	common selfheal
	Pycnanthemum incanum	hoary mountainmint
	Pycnanthemum tenuifolium	narrowleaf mountainmint
	Pycnanthemum verticillatum var. *verticillatum*	whorled mountainmint
	Pycnanthemum virginianum	Virginia mountainmint
	Teucrium canadense	Canada germander
Lauraceae	*Lindera benzoin*	northern spicebush
	Sassafras albidum	sassafras
Lemnaceae	*Lemna* sp.	duckweed
Liliaceae	*Allium canadense*	meadow garlic
	Allium vineale	wild garlic
	Hemerocallis fulva	orange daylily
	Hypoxis hirsuta	common goldstar
	Lilium canadense	Canada lily
	Lilium sp.	lily
	Maianthemum canadense	Canada mayflower
	Maianthemum racemosum	feathery false lily of the valley

Family	Latin name	Common name
Liliaceae (cont)	*Medeola virginiana*	Indian cucumber
	Polygonatum biflorum	smooth Solomon's seal
	Polygonatum pubescens	hairy Solomon's seal
	Trillium cernuum	whip-poor-will flower
	Uvularia perfoliata	perfoliate bellwort
	Uvularia sessilifolia	sessileleaf bellwort
	Veratrum viride	green false hellebore
Lycopodiaceae	*Lycopodium digitatum*	fan clubmoss
	Lycopodium obscurum	rare clubmoss
Lythraceae	*Lythrum salicaria*	purple loosestrife
Magnoliaceae	*Liriodendron tulipifera*	tuliptree
Menispermaceae	*Menispermum canadense*	common moonseed
Monotropaceae	*Monotropa uniflora*	Indianpipe
Moraceae	*Morus alba*	white mulberry
Myricaceae	*Comptonia peregrina*	sweet fern
Oleaceae	*Fraxinus americana*	white ash
	Fraxinus pennsylvanica	green ash
	Fraxinus sp.	ash
	Ligustrum sp.	privet
Onagraceae	*Circaea lutetiana*	broadleaf enchanter's nightshade
	Oenothera fruticosa	narrowleaf evening-primrose
Ophioglossaceae	*Botrychium virginianum*	rattlesnake fern
Orchidaceae	*Cypripedium acaule*	moccasin flower
	Epipactis helleborine	broadleaf helleborine
	Goodyera pubescens	downy rattlesnake plantain
	Isotria verticillata	large whorled pogonia
	Spiranthes sp.	lady's tresses
Osmundaceae	*Osmunda cinnamomea*	cinnamon fern
	Osmunda claytoniana	interrupted fern
	Osmunda sp.	osmunda
Oxalidaceae	*Oxalis* sp.	woodsorrel
	Oxalis stricta	common yellow oxalis
Papaveraceae	*Chelidonium majus*	celandine
	Sanguinaria canadensis	bloodroot
	Stylophorum diphyllum	celandine poppy
Phytolaccaceae	*Phytolacca americana*	American pokeweed
Pinaceae	*Picea abies*	Norway spruce
	Pinus rigida	pitch pine
	Pinus sp.	pine
	Pinus strobus	eastern white pine
	Tsuga canadensis	eastern hemlock
Plantaginaceae	*Plantago lanceolata*	narrowleaf plantain
Platanaceae	*Platanus occidentalis*	American sycamore
Poaceae	*Agrostis gigantea*	redtop
	Agrostis sp.	bentgrass
	Anthoxanthum odoratum	sweet vernalgrass
	Brachyelytrum erectum	bearded shorthusk
	Bromus inermis	smooth brome
	Bromus pubescens	hairy woodland brome
	Danthonia spicata	poverty oatgrass
	Deschampsia flexuosa	wavy hairgrass
	Dichanthelium acuminatum	tapered rosette grass
	Dichanthelium boscii	Bosc's panicgrass
	Dichanthelium clandestinum	deertongue
	Dichanthelium commutatum	variable panicgrass
	Dichanthelium depauperatum	starved panicgrass
	Dichanthelium dichotomum	cypress panicgrass
	Dichanthelium linearifolium	slimleaf panicgrass
	Dichanthelium sp.	rosette grass
	Elymus hystrix	eastern bottlebrush grass
	Elymus repens	quackgrass

Family	Latin name	Common name
Poaceae (cont)	*Elymus riparius*	riverbank wildrye
	Elymus sp.	wildrye
	Eragrostis pectinacea	tufted lovegrass
	Festuca rubra	red fescue
	Festuca subverticillata	nodding fescue
	Glyceria melicaria	melic mannagrass
	Glyceria sp.	mannagrass
	Glyceria striata	fowl mannagrass
	Holcus lanatus	common velvetgrass
	Leersia oryzoides	rice cutgrass
	Leersia virginica	whitegrass
	Microstegium vimineum	Japanese stiltgrass
	Muhlenbergia sobolifera	rock muhly
	Phalaris arundinacea	reed canarygrass
	Phleum pratense	timothy
	Poa alsodes	grove bluegrass
	Poa compressa	Canada bluegrass
	Poa nemoralis	wood bluegrass
	Poa pratensis	Kentucky bluegrass
	Poa saltuensis	oldpasture bluegrass
	Poa sp.	bluegrass
	Poa sylvestris	woodland bluegrass
	Poa trivialis	rough bluegrass
	Schizachyrium scoparium	little bluestem
	Sphenopholis intermedia	slender wedgescale
Polemoniaceae	*Phlox subulata*	moss phlox
Polygalaceae	*Polygala paucifolia*	gaywings
Polygonaceae	*Polygonum amphibium*	water knotweed
	Polygonum caespitosum	Oriental ladysthumb
	Polygonum convolvulus	black bindweed
	Polygonum cuspidatum	Japanese knotweed
	Polygonum hydropiper	marshpepper knotweed
	Polygonum sagittatum	arrowleaf tearthumb
	Polygonum scandens	climbing false buckwheat
	Polygonum sp.	knotweed
	Polygonum virginianum	jumpseed
	Rumex acetosella	common sheep sorrel
	Rumex obtusifolius	bitter dock
	Rumex sp.	dock
Polypodiaceae	*Polypodium* sp.	polypody
	Polypodium virginianum	rock polypody
Primulaceae	*Lysimachia ciliata*	fringed loosestrife
	Lysimachia quadrifolia	whorled yellow loosestrife
	Trientalis borealis	starflower
Pteridaceae	*Adiantum pedatum*	northern maidenhair
Pyrolaceae	*Chimaphila maculata*	striped prince's pine
	Pyrola elliptica	waxflower shinleaf
	Pyrola sp.	wintergreen
Ranunculaceae	*Actaea pachypoda*	white baneberry
	Actaea racemosa	black baneberry
	Anemone quinquefolia	wood anemone
	Aquilegia canadensis	red columbine
	Clematis sp.	leather flower
	Clematis virginiana	devil's darning needles
	Delphinium tricorne	dwarf larkspur
	Hepatica nobilis var. *obtusa*	roundlobe hepatica
	Ranunculus abortivus	littleleaf buttercup
	Ranunculus recurvatus	blisterwort
	Ranunculus sardous	hairy buttercup
	Ranunculus sceleratus	cursed buttercup
	Ranunculus sp.	buttercup

Family	Latin name	Common name
Ranunculaceae (cont)	*Thalictrum dioicum*	early meadow-rue
	Thalictrum pubescens	king of the meadow
	Thalictrum sp.	meadow-rue
Rosaceae	*Agrimonia* sp.	agrimony
	Amelanchier arborea	common serviceberry
	Crataegus sp.	hawthorn
	Duchesnea indica	Indian strawberry
	Fragaria virginiana	Virginia strawberry
	Geum canadense	white avens
	Geum laciniatum	rough avens
	Geum sp.	avens
	Malus sp.	apple
	Photinia melanocarpa	black chokeberry
	Potentilla canadensis	dwarf cinquefoil
	Potentilla simplex	common cinquefoil
	Potentilla sp.	cinquefoil
	Prunus avium	sweet cherry
	Prunus serotina	black cherry
	Prunus sp.	plum
	Rosa carolina	Carolina rose
	Rosa multiflora	multiflora rose
	Rubus allegheniensis	Allegheny blackberry
	Rubus flagellaris	northern dewberry
	Rubus hispidus	bristly dewberry
	Rubus occidentalis	black raspberry
	Rubus phoenicolasius	wine raspberry
	Rubus sp.	blackberry
	Spiraea alba	white meadowsweet
	Spiraea alba var. *latifolia*	white meadowsweet
Rubiaceae	*Cruciata pedemontana*	piedmont bedstraw
	Galium aparine	stickywilly
	Galium asprellum	rough bedstraw
	Galium circaezans	licorice bedstraw
	Galium lanceolatum	lanceleaf wild licorice
	Galium mollugo	false baby's breath
	Galium sp.	bedstraw
	Galium tinctorium	stiff marsh bedstraw
	Galium triflorum	fragrant bedstraw
	Houstonia caerulea	azure bluet
	Mitchella repens	partridgeberry
Salicaceae	*Populus grandidentata*	bigtooth aspen
	Populus tremuloides	quaking aspen
Santalaceae	*Comandra umbellata*	bastard toadflax
Saxifragaceae	*Mitella diphylla*	twoleaf miterwort
Scrophulariaceae	*Digitalis lutea*	straw foxglove
	Linaria vulgaris	butter and eggs
	Melampyrum lineare	narrowleaf cowwheat
	Mimulus ringens	Allegheny monkeyflower
	Mimulus sp.	monkeyflower
	Penstemon digitalis	talus slope penstemon
	Penstemon sp.	beardtongue
	Scrophularia lanceolata	lanceleaf figwort
	Scrophularia sp.	figwort
	Verbascum thapsus	common mullein
	Veronica anagallis-aquatica	water speedwell
	Veronica officinalis	common gypsyweed
Simaroubaceae	*Ailanthus altissima*	tree of heaven
Smilacaceae	*Smilax glauca*	cat greenbrier
	Smilax herbacea	smooth carrionflower
	Smilax rotundifolia	roundleaf greenbrier
	Smilax sp.	greenbrier

Family	Latin name	Common name
Solanaceae	*Physalis heterophylla*	clammy groundcherry
	Solanum carolinense	Carolina horsenettle
	Solanum sp.	nightshade
Staphyleaceae	*Staphylea trifolia*	American bladdernut
Thelypteridaceae	*Phegopteris connectilis*	long beechfern
	Phegopteris hexagonoptera	broad beechfern
	Thelypteris noveboracensis	New York fern
	Thelypteris palustris	eastern marsh fern
Tiliaceae	*Tilia americana*	American basswood
Typhaceae	*Typha angustifolia*	narrowleaf cattail
Ulmaceae	*Celtis occidentalis*	common hackberry
	Ulmus americana	American elm
	Ulmus rubra	slippery elm
	Ulmus sp.	elm
Urticaceae	*Boehmeria cylindrica*	smallspike false nettle
	Laportea canadensis	Canadian woodnettle
	Pilea pumila	Canadian clearweed
	Urtica dioica	stinging nettle
Verbenaceae	*Phryma leptostachya*	American lopseed
	Verbena hastata	swamp verbena
	Verbena urticifolia	white vervain
Violaceae	*Hybanthus concolor*	eastern greenviolet
	Viola blanda	sweet white violet
	Viola labradorica	alpine violet
	Viola pubescens	downy yellow violet
	Viola rotundifolia	roundleaf yellow violet
	Viola sagittata	arrowleaf violet
	Viola sagittata var. *ovata*	arrowleaf violet
	Viola sororia	common blue violet
	Viola sp.	violet
	Viola striata	striped cream violet
Vitaceae	*Parthenocissus quinquefolia*	Virginia creeper
	Vitis aestivalis	summer grape
	Vitis labrusca	fox grape
	Vitis riparia	riverbank grape
	Vitis sp.	grape

NPS 620/101469, March 2010